Revolution and Romanticism, 1789-1834
A series of facsimile reprints chosen and introduced by
Jonathan Wordsworth
University Lecturer in Romantic Studies at Oxford

Wollstonecraft
Thoughts on the education of daughters 1787

Mary Wollstonecraft

Thoughts on the education of daughters
1787

Woodstock Books
Oxford and New York
1994

This edition first published 1994 by
Woodstock Books
Spelsbury House, Spelsbury, Oxford OX7 3JR
and
Woodstock Books
387 Park Avenue South
New York, NY 10016-8810

ISBN 1 85477 195 7
New matter copyright © Woodstock Books 1994

British Library Cataloguing in Publication Data
A catalogue record for this book is
available from the British Library

Library of Congress Cataloging-in-Publication Data
Wollstonecraft, Mary, 1759-1797.
    Thoughts on the education of daughters / Mary
    Wollstonecraft.
        p. cm. – (Revolution and romanticism, 1789-1834)
    Originally published: London: J. Johnson, 1787.
    ISBN 1-85477-195-7: $48.00
    1. Young women.   2. Women – Conduct of life.   I. Title.
    II. Series.
    HQ1229.W85   1994
    305.42–dc20
                                                    94-5545
                                                    CIP

Printed and bound in Great Britain by
Smith Settle
Otley, West Yorkshire LS21 3JP

Introduction

Wollstonecraft did not provide *Thoughts on the education of
daughters* with a Table of Contents, but a glance at the list
she might have included tells us a good deal about the
book. Aside from beginning in the nursery, she appears
not to be interested in structure. Though Wollstonecraft
and her sisters have for two years been running a school,
education here plainly has nothing to do with a
curriculum. Implied in the listed headings is a decided
moral emphasis: manners are artificial, disappointments
beneficial; by implication, principles should be steady,
Sunday should be observed, we are to practise
benevolence and think twice about card-playing.
Standing out from other headings by virtue of its length
and personal tone (and unintended pun) is 'Unfortunate
Situation Of Females, Fashionably Educated, But Left
Without A Fortune'. This is not, it seems, an egalitarian
work – and not one that is written from an entirely
detached position.

Wollstonecraft's overall title, of course, suggests that
her book is a sequel to Locke, *Some thoughts concerning
education* (1693). In print at least, Locke had ignored the
existence of girls; Wollstonecraft, in the enlightened 1780s,
would give them their due. But if this was indeed her
intention, she soon found how hard it was to achieve. Her
sole reference to Locke occurs on page eleven:

To be able to follow Mr Locke's system (and this may be said of almost all treatises on education) the parents must have subdued their own passions, which is not often the case in any considerable degree.

The marriage state is too often a state of discord; it does not always happen that both parents are rational, and the weakest have it in their power to do most mischief.

How then are the tender minds of children to be cultivated? – Mamma is only anxious that they should love her best, and perhaps takes pains to sow those seeds which have produced such luxuriant weeds in her own mind. Or, what still more frequently occurs, the children are at first made playthings of, and when their tempers have been spoiled by indiscreet indulgence, they become troublesome, and are mostly left with servants; the first notions they imbibe, therefore, are mean and vulgar. They are taught cunning, the wisdom of that class of people, and a love of truth, the foundation of virtue, is soon obliterated from their minds.

To which Wollstonecraft adds, in what can only be an assertion of freedom from Locke, 'It is, in my opinion, a well-proved fact, that principles of truth are innate.' Abetted by their servants (about whom Wollstonecraft is consistently harsh), parents are destroying the love of truth with which the child is born. It is sort of counter-education. A similar process will turn to evil the innately good Creature in her daughter's novel, *Frankenstein*.

Locke, by contrast, had written his *Thoughts* as an aid to friends (both of them rational), who were anxious to do all that was right for their son. Deciding to publish, he not surprisingly put the work in a larger, more idealistic context:

The well Educating of their Children is so much the Duty and Concern of Parents, and the Welfare and Prosperity of the Nation so much depends on it, that I would have every one lay it seriously to Heart, and ... set his Helping Hand to promote every where that Way of training up Youth, with regard to their several

Conditions, which is the easiest, shortest, and likeliest to produce vertuous, useful, and able Men in their distinct Callings.

For a moment we are permitted the thought that all classes will be catered for, because all can be 'vertuous, useful, and able'. Locke, however, tells us firmly 'the Gentleman's Calling' is

most to be taken care of … For if those of that Rank are by their Education once set right, they will quickly bring all the rest into Order.

(*Educational writings*, ed. Axtell, 112-13)

Adapted to a non-hereditary elite, Locke's faith reappears 100 years later in Godwin's *Political justice*:

Infuse just views of society into a certain number of the liberally educated and reflecting members; give to the people guides and instructors; and the business is done.

(1793 *Political justice* i, 69)

Wollstonecraft in *Vidication of the rights of woman* (1792) is Lockean too in this respect, arguing the case for female education (a year before her future husband's treatise) on the grounds that women should naturally be the educators. Having in their charge both the males and the females of future generations, they are uniquely placed to bring about social change. *Thoughts on the education of daughters* does not arrive at this point. Written as it is at Stoke Newington, under the eyes of Richard Price, it accepts the positions (Lockean in origin) of rational dissent: 'Universal benevolence is the first duty' (p. 91). But neither the political scene, nor Wollstonecraft's own life, gives cause in 1786 for optimism. So far from addressing herself to Locke's well-intentioned and intelligent parents, willing to give time and thought to their offspring, she takes it for granted that they will be uncaring. 'Mamma is only anxious that [the children] should love her best'; Papa is ineffectual, maybe worse.

Locke patiently constructs an ideal. Not until his work had been drafted was he asked how the Clarkes should bring up their two daughters. Then, in a letter of February 1685, he suggests for them the same education as their brother. His views in general are amazingly enlightened:

None of the Things they [children] are to learn should ever be made a Burthen to them, or imposed on them as a *Task*. (Axtell, 172)

It will perhaps be wondered that I mentioned *Reasoning* with Children: And yet I cannot but think that the true Way of Dealing with them. (*ibid*, 181)

Beating is the worst, and therefore the last Means to be used in the Correction of Children; and that only in Cases of Extremity, after all gentler Ways have been tried, and proved unsuccessful. (*ibid*, 183)

As Children's *Enquiries* are not to be slighted, so also great care is to be taken that they *never* receive *Deceitful* and *Eluding Answers*. (ibid, 230)

Thoughts on the education of daughters belongs to a different world. It takes the form of a manual, but is in truth a protest against contemporary society. Wollstonecraft may set out to offer advice comparable to Locke's – 'whenever a child asks a question, it should always have a reasonable answer given it' – but her sense of the disastrous current situation makes it impossible to stay on the level of practical suggestions.

Wollstonecraft's instinct is to fight. With Pope, for instance, who has stereotyped women as coquettes in the *Rape of the lock*, and famously denied them character in *Epistle to a lady*. But even as she comes back at him – 'there are quite as many male coquets as female, and they are far more pernicious pests to society' (p. 81); 'Most women, and men too, have no character at all' (p. 111) – we feel that she is close to sharing his view. The women of whom she writes are at once trapped and collusive. Mamma has had little opportunity, and no encouragement, to become rational. Treated as a plaything herself in the nursery, she has been briefly exiled to the kitchen, then packed off to a boarding school, where 'few things are learnt thoroughly, but many follies contracted, and an immoderate fondness for dress among the rest' (p. 58). Leaving school, she has no other aim but marriage. 'Scarcely out of the state of childhood herself', she is 'placed at the head of a family' (p. 96). If she perpetuates the faults of her own upbringing it is little wonder.

As a female 'fashionably educated and left without a fortune', Wollstonecraft too is in a trap. With all her reservations about the married state, it is painful to be unmarriageable. Of the few jobs available to women in her situation – paid companion, school-teacher, governess – she has tried the first two, and will soon try the third. All are humiliating. 'It is impossible to enumerate the many hours of anguish such a person must spend', she wrote of being a companion:

Painfully sensible of unkindness, she is alive to every thing, and many sarcasms reach her, which were perhaps directed another way. She is alone, shut out from equality and confidence, and the concealed anxiety impairs her constitution; for she must wear a cheerful face, or be dismissed. (p. 71)

As writer too, Woolstonecraft is trapped. Unable to see a way out of the cycle of indulgent mother, spoiled child, indulgent mother, she is compelled nevertheless to think of education in terms of marriage:

To prepare a woman to fulfil the important duties of wife and mother, are certainly the objects that should be in view during the early period of life. (p. 58)

It is for this reason that *Thoughts on the education of daughters* increasingly draws the reader's attention to the love of God: 'He who has made us must know what will tend to our ultimate good' (p. 107). If not on earth, everything will be put right in 'that world *where there is neither marrying*, nor giving in marriage' (final words of *Mary, a fiction*, 1788).

Already in this her first book it is clear that the strength of Wollstonecraft's writing lies in determined personality and a refusal to accept what she sees to be wrong. She has yet to develop the more cutting tones of the second *Vindication* – 'I have, probably, had an opportunity of observing more girls in their infancy than J.J. Rousseau' (he put his children at birth, one recalls, into a Foundling Hospital) – but she is very much herself. She has found her cause. The women she sees about her are not easy to fight for, but fight she will.

J. W.

THOUGHTS

ON THE

EDUCATION

OF

DAUGHTERS:

WITH

REFLECTIONS ON FEMALE CONDUCT,

IN

The more important DUTIES of LIFE.

By MARY WOLLSTONECRAFT.

———————

LONDON:

PRINTED FOR J. JOHNSON, Nº 72, ST. PAUL'S
CHURCH-YARD.

M DCC LXXXVII.

PREFACE.

IN the following pages I have endeavoured to point out some important things with respect to female education. It is true, many treatises have been already written; yet it occurred to me, that much still remained to be said. I shall not swell these sheets by writing apologies for my attempt. I am afraid, indeed, the reflections will, by some, be thought too grave; but I could not make them less so without writing af-

3   fectedly;

fectedly; yet, though they may be insipid to the gay, others may not think them so; and if they should prove useful to one fellow-creature, and beguile any hours, which sorrow has made heavy, I shall think I have not been employed in vain.

THOUGHTS

THOUGHTS

ON THE

EDUCATION

OF

DAUGHTERS.

THE NURSERY.

AS I conceive it to be the duty of
every rational creature to attend to its offspring, I am sorry to observe, that reason and duty together
have not so powerful an influence over
human

human conduct, as inftinct has in the brute creation. Indolence, and a thoughtlefs difregard of every thing, except the prefent indulgence, make many mothers, who may have momentary ftarts of tendernefs, neglect their children. They follow a pleafing impulfe, and never reflect that reafon fhould cultivate and govern thofe inftincts which are implanted in us to render the path of duty pleafant—for if they are not governed they will run wild; and ftrengthen the paffions which are ever endeavouring to obtain dominion—I mean vanity and felf-love.

The

The firſt thing to be attended to, is laying the foundation of a good conſtitution. The mother (if there are not very weighty reaſons to prevent her) ought to ſuckle her children. Her milk is their proper nutriment, and for ſome time is quite ſufficient. Were a regular mode of ſuckling adopted, it would be far from being a laborious taſk. Children, who are left to the care of ignorant nurſes, have their ſtomachs overloaded with improper food, which turns acid, and renders them very uncomfortable. We ſhould be particularly careful to guard them in their infant ſtate from bodily pain; as their minds can then afford them no

amuſe-

amusement to alleviate it. The first years of a child's life are frequently made miserable through negligence or ignorance. Their complaints are mostly in their stomach or bowels; and these complaints generally arise from the quality and quantity of their food.

The suckling of a child also excites the warmest glow of tenderness—Its dependant, helpless state produces an affection, which may properly be termed maternal. I have even felt it, when I have seen a mother perform that office; and am of opinion, that maternal tenderness arises quite as much from habit as instinct. It is possible, I

m

am convinced, to acquire the affection
of a parent for an adopted child; it is
neceſſary, therefore, for a mother to
perform the office of one, in order to
produce in herſelf a rational affection
for her offspring.

Children very early contract the
manners of thoſe about them. It is
eaſy to diſtinguiſh the child of a well-
bred perſon, if it is not left entirely to
the nurſe's care. Theſe women are
of courſe ignorant, and to keep a child
quiet for the moment, they humour
all its little caprices. Very ſoon does
it begin to be perverſe, and eager to
be gratified in every thing. The uſual

B 3   mode

mode of acting is complying with the
humours sometimes, and contradicting
them at others—just according to the
dictates of an uncorrected temper.
This the infant finds out earlier than
can be imagined, and it gives rise to
an affection devoid of respect. Uni-
formity of conduct is the only feasible
method of creating both. An inflexi-
ble adherence to any rule that has
been laid down makes children comfortable, and saves the mother and
nurse much trouble, as they will not
often contest, if they have not once
conquered. They will, I am sure,
love and respect a person who treats
them properly, if some one else does

not

not indiscreetly indulge them. I once heard a judicious father say, " He would treat his child as he would his horse : first convince it he was its master, and then its friend." But yet a rigid style of behaviour is by no means to be adopted; on the contrary, I wish to remark, that it is only in the years of childhood that the happiness of a human being depends entirely on others—and to embitter those years by needless restraint is cruel. To conciliate affection, affection must be shown, and little proofs of it ought always to be given—let them not appear weaknesses, and they will sink deep into the young mind, and call

forth

forth its most amiable propensities. The turbulent passions may be kept down till reason begins to dawn.

In the nursery too, they are taught to speak; and there they not only hear nonsense, but that nonsense retailed out in such silly, affected tones as must disgust;—yet these are the tones which the child first imitates, and its innocent playful manner renders them tolerable, if not pleasing; but afterwards they are not easily got the better of—nay, many women always retain the pretty prattle of the nursery, and do not forget to lisp, when they have learnt to languish.

Children

Children are taught revenge and lies in their very cradles. If they fall down, or ſtrike their heads againſt any thing, to quiet them they are bid return the injury, and their little hands held out to do it. When they cry, or are troubleſome, the cat or dog is chaſtiſed, or ſome bugbear called to take them away; which only terrifies them at firſt, for they ſoon find out that the nurſe means nothing by theſe dreadful threatenings. Indeed, ſo well do they diſcover the fallacy, that I have ſeen little creatures, who could ſcarcely ſpeak, play over the ſame tricks with their doll or the cat.

How,

How, then, when the mind comes under diſcipline, can precepts of truth be inforced, when the firſt examples they have had would lead them to practiſe the contrary?

MORAL

MORAL DISCIPLINE.

IT has been afferted, " That no be-ing, merely human, could properly educate a child." I entirely coincide with this author; but though perfec-tion cannot be attained, and unfore-feen events will ever govern human conduct, yet ftill it is our duty to lay down fome rule to regulate our ac-tions by, and to adhere to it, as confift-ently as our infirmities will permit. To be able to follow Mr. Locke's fyf-tem (and this may be faid of almoft all treatifes on education) the parents muft have fubdued their own paffions, which

which is not often the cafe in any confiderable degree.

The marriage ftate is too often a
ftate of difcord; it does not always
happen that both parents are rational,
and the weakeft have it in their power
to do moft mifchief.

How then are the tender minds
of children to be cultivated?—
Mamma is only anxious that they
fhould love her beft, and perhaps
takes pains to fow thofe feeds,
which have produced fuch luxuriant
weeds in her own mind. Or, what ftill
more frequently occurs, the children
are at firft made play-things of, and
when

when their tempers have been spoiled by indiscreet indulgence, they become troublesome, and are mostly left with servants; the first notions they imbibe, therefore, are mean and vulgar. They are taught cunning, the wisdom of that class of people, and a love of truth, the foundation of virtue, is soon obliterated from their minds. It is, in my opinion, a well-proved fact, that principles of truth are innate. Without reasoning we assent to many truths; we feel their force, and artful sophistry can only blunt those feelings which nature has implanted in us as instinctive guards to virtue. Dissimulation and cunning will soon drive all other good

good qualities before them, and de-
prive the mind of that beautiful fim-
plicity, which can never be too much
cherifhed.

Indeed it is of the utmoft confequence to make a child artlefs, or to
fpeak with more propriety, not to
teach them to be otherwife; and in
order to do fo we muft keep them out
of the way of bad examples. Art is
almoft always practifed by fervants,
and the fame methods which children
obferve them to ufe, to fhield themfelves from blame, they will adopt—
and cunning is fo nearly allied to falfe-
hood, that it will infallibly lead to it—

or some foolish prevaricating subter-
fuge will occur, to silence any re-
proaches of the mind which may arise,
if an attention to truth has been inculcated.

Another cause or source of art is in-
judicious correction. Accidents or
giddy tricks are too frequently pu-
nished, and if children can conceal
these, they will, to avoid chastisement.
Restrain them, therefore, but never
correct them without a very sufficient
cause; such as a violation of truth,
cruelty to animals, inferiors, or those
kind of follies which lead to vice.

Children

Children fhould be permitted to enter into converfation; but it requires
great difcernment to find out fuch
fubjects as will gradually improve
them. Animals are the firft objects
which catch their attention; and I
think little ftories about them would
not only amufe but inftruct at the fame
time, and have the beft effect in forming the temper and cultivating the
good difpofitions of the heart. There
are many little books which have
this tendency. One in particular I
recollect: The Perambulations of a
Moufe. I cannot here help mentioning a book of hymns, in meafured
profe, written by the ingenious author

of

of many other proper leſſons for children. Theſe hymns, I imagine, would
contribute to fill the heart with religious ſentiments and affections; and,
if I may be allowed the expreſſion,
make the Deity obvious to the ſenſes.
The underſtanding, however, ſhould
not be overloaded any more than the
ſtomach. Intellectual improvements,
like the growth and formation of the
body, muſt be gradual—yet there is no
reaſon why the mind ſhould lie fallow,
while its " frail tenement" is imperceptibly fitting itſelf for a more rea-
ſonable inhabitant. It will not lie fallow; promiſcuous ſeeds will be ſown
by accident, and they will ſhoot up

C with

with the wheat, and perhaps never be eradicated.

Whenever a child afks a queftion, it fhould always have a reafonable anfwer given it. Its little paffions fhould be engaged. They are moftly fond of ftories, and proper ones would improve them even while they are amufed. Inftead of thefe, their heads are filled with improbable tales, and fuperftitious accounts of invifible beings, which breed ftrange prejudices and vain fears in their minds.

The lifp of the nurfery is confirmed, and vulgar phrafes are acquired; which children, if poffible, fhould never hear.

3   To

To be able to expreſs the thoughts with facility and propriety, is of great conſequence in life, and if children were never led aſtray in this particular, it would prevent much trouble.

The riot too of the kitchen, or any other place where children are left only with ſervants, makes the decent reſtraint of the parlour irkſome. A girl, who has vivacity, ſoon grows a romp ; and if there are male ſervants, they go out a walking with them, and will frequently take little freedoms with Miſs, the bearing with which gives a forwardneſs to her air, and makes her pert. The becoming mo-

deſty.

defty, which being accuftomed to converfe with fuperiors, will give a girl,
is entirely done away.   I muft own,
I am quite charmed when I fee a fweet
young creature, fhrinking as it were
from obfervation, and liftening rather
than talking.   It is poffible a girl may
have this manner without having a very
good underftanding.   If it fhould be
fo, this diffidence prevents her from
being troublefome.

It is the duty of a parent to preferve
a child from receiving wrong impref-
fions.—As to prejudices, the firft notions we have deferve that name; for
it is not till we begin to waver in our
opinions,

opinions, that we exert our reafon to examine them——and then, if they are received, they may be called our own.

The firft things, then, that children ought to be encouraged to obferve, are a ftrict adherence to truth; a proper fubmiffion to fuperiors; and condefcenfion to inferiors. Thefe are the main articles; but there are many others, which compared to them are trivial, and yet are of importance. It is not pleafing to fee a child full of bows and grimaces; yet they need not be fuffered to be rude. They fhould be employed, and fuch fables and tales may be culled out for them as would

C 3   excite

excite their curiofity.   A tafte for the
beauties of nature fhould be very early
cultivated : many things, with refpect
to the vegetable and animal world,
may be explained in an amufing way ;
and this is an innocent fource of pleafure within every one's reach.

Above all, try to teach them to
combine their ideas.   It is of more ufe
than can be conceived, for a child to
learn to compare things that are fimilar in fome refpects, and different in
others.   I wifh them to be taught to
think—thinking, indeed, is a fevere
exercife, and exercife of either mind or
body will not at firft be entered on, but
                                   with

with a view to pleasure. Not that I would have them make long reflections; for when they do not arise from experience, they are mostly absurd.

EX-

EXTERIOR ACCOMPLISH-
MENTS.

UNDER this head may be ranked all thofe accomplifhments which merely render the perfon attractive; and thofe half-learnt ones which do not improve the mind. "A little learning of any kind is a dangerous thing;" and fo far from making a perfon pleafing, it has the contrary effect.

Parents have moftly fome weighty weighty bufinefs in hand, which they make a pretext to themfelves for neglecting the arduous tafk of educating their children; they are therefore fent

8   to

to fchool, and the allowance for them is fo low, that the perfon who undertakes the charge muft have more than fhe can poffibly attend to; of courfe, the mechanical parts of education can only be obferved.   I have known children who could repeat things in the order they learnt them, that were quite at a lofs when put out of the beaten track.   If the underftanding is not exercifed, the memory will be employed to little purpofe.

Girls learn fomething of mufic, drawing, and geography; but they do not know enough to engage their attention, and render it an employment of the mind.   If they can play over a few

tunes

tunes to their acquaintance, and have a drawing or two (half done by the master) to hang up in their rooms, they imagine themselves artists for the rest of their lives. It is not the being able to execute a trifling landscape, or any thing of the kind, that is of consequence—These are at best but trifles, and the foolish, indiscriminate praises which are bestowed on them only produce vanity. But what is really of no importance, when considered in this light, becomes of the utmost, when a girl has a fondness for the art, and a desire of excellence. Whatever tends to make a person in some measure independent

of

of the fenfes, is a prop to virtue. A-
mufing employments muft firft occupy
the mind ; and as an attention to moral duties leads to piety, fo whoever
weighs one fubject will turn to others,
and new ideas will rufh into the mind.
The faculties will be exercifed, and
not fuffered to fleep, which will give a
variety to the character.

Dancing and elegance of manners
are very pleafing, if too great a ftrefs
is not laid on them. Thefe acquire-
ments catch the fenfes, and open the
way to the heart ; but unfupported by
folid good qualities, their reign is fhort.

The lively thoughtleffnefs of youth
makes every young creature agreeable
for]

for the time; but when those years are flown, and sense is not substituted in the stead of vivacity, the follies of youth are acted over, and they never consider, that the things which please in their proper season, disgust out of it. It is very absurd to see a woman, whose brow time has marked with wrinkles, aping the manners of a girl in her teens.

I do not think it foreign to the present subject to mention the trifling conversations women are mostly fond of. In general, they are prone to ridicule. As they lay the greatest stress on manners, the most respectable characters

will

will not efcape its lafh, if deficient in
this article. Ridicule has been, with
fome people, the boafted teft of truth
—if fo, our fex ought to make won-
derful improvements; but I am apt to
think, they often exert this talent till
they lofe all perception of it themfelves.
Affectation, and not ignorance, is the
fair game for ridicule; and even affectation fome good-natured perfons
will fpare. We fhould never give pain
without a defign to amend.

Exterior accomplifhments are not to
be defpifed, if the acquiring of them
does not fatisfy the poffeffors, and prevent their cultivating the more important ones.

ARTI-

ARTIFICIAL MANNERS.

IT may be thought, that artificial manners and exterior accomplishments are much the same; but I think the former take a far wider range, and are materially different. The one arises from affectation, and the other seems only an error in judgment.

The emotions of the mind often appear conspicuous in the countenance and manner. These emotions, when they arise from sensibility and virtue, are inexpressibly pleasing. But it is easier to copy the cast of countenance, than to cultivate the virtues which animate and improve it.

How

How many people are like whitened sepulchres, and careful only about appearances! yet if we are too anxious to gain the approbation of the world, we muſt often forfeit our own.

How bewitching is that humble ſoftneſs of manners which humility gives birth to, and how faint are the imitations of affectation! That gentleneſs of behaviour, which makes us courteous to all, and that benevolence, which makes us loth to offend any, and ſtudious to pleaſe every creature, is ſometimes copied by the polite; but how aukward is the copy! The warmeſt profeſſions of regard are proſtituted

tituted on all occafions. No diftinc-
tions are made, and the efteem which
is only due to merit, appears to be
lavifhed on all—Nay, affection is affected; at leaft, the language is bor-
rowed, when there is no glow of it in
the heart. Civility is due to all, but
regard or admiration fhould never be
expreffed when it is not felt.

As humility gives the moft pleafing
caft to the countenance, fo from fin-
cerity arifes that artleffnefs of manners
which is fo engaging. She who fuf-
fers herfelf to be feen as fhe really is,
can never be thought affected. She
is not folicitous to act a part; her en-

deavour

deavour is not to hide; but correct
her failings, and her face has of courſe
that beauty, which an attention to the
mind only gives. I never knew a perſon really ugly, who was not fooliſh
or vicious; and I have ſeen the moſt
beautiful features deformed by paſſion
and vice. It is true, regular features
ſtrike at firſt; but it is a well ordered
mind which occaſions thoſe turns of
expreſſion in the countenance, which
make a laſting impreſſion.

Feeling is ridiculous when affected;
and even when felt, ought not to be
diſplayed. It will appear if genuine;
but when puſhed forward to notice, it
is obvious vanity has rivalled ſorrow,

and

and that the prettinefs of the thing is thought of. Let the manners arife from the mind, and let there be no difguife for the genuine emotions of the heart.

Things merely ornamental are foon difregarded, and difregard can fcarcely be borne when there is no internal fupport.

To have in this uncertain world fome ftay, which cannot be undermined, is of the utmoft confequence ; and this ftay it is, which gives that dignity to the manners, which fhews that a perfon does not depend on mere human applaufe for comfort and fatisfaction.

DRESS.

D R E S S.

MANY able pens have dwelt on
the peculiar foibles of our fex.
We have been equally defired to avoid
the two extremes in drefs, and the ne-
ceffity of cleanlinefs has been infifted
on, " As from the body's purity the
mind receives a fympathetic aid."

By far too much of a girl's time is
taken up in drefs. This is an exterior
accomplifhment; but I chofe to confider it by itfelf. The body hides the
mind, and it is, in its turn, obfcured
by the drapery. I hate to fee the
frame of a picture fo glaring, as to

D 2   catch

catch the eye and divide the attention. Dreſs ought to adorn the perſon, and not rival it. It may be ſimple, elegant, and becoming, without being expenſive; and ridiculous faſhions diſregarded, while ſingularity is avoided. The beauty of dreſs (I ſhall raiſe aſtoniſhment by ſaying ſo) is its not being conſpicuous one way or the other; when it neither diſtorts, or hides the human form by unnatural protuberances. If ornaments are much ſtudied, a conſciouſneſs of being well dreſſed will appear in the face—and ſurely this mean pride does not give much ſublimity to it.

" Out

" Out of the abundance of the heart the mouth fpeaketh." And how much converfation does drefs furnifh, which furely cannot be very improving or entertaining.

It gives rife to envy, and contefts for trifling fuperiority, which do not render a woman very refpectable to the other fex.

Arts are ufed to obtain money; and much is fquandered away, which if faved for charitable purpofes, might alleviate the diftrefs of many poor families, and foften the heart of the girl who entered into fuch fcenes of woe.

D 3

In

In the article of dress may be included the whole tribe of beauty-washes, cosmetics, Olympian dew, oriental herbs, liquid bloom, and the paint which enlivened Ninon's face, and bid defiance to time. These numerous and essential articles are advertised in so ridiculous a style, that the rapid sale of them is a very severe reflection on the understanding of those females who encourage it. The dew and herbs, I imagine, are very harmless, but I do not know whether the same may be said of the paint. White is certainly very prejudicial to the health, and never can be made to resemble nature. The red, too, takes

off from the expression of the countenance, and the beautiful glow which
modesty, affection, or any other emotion of the mind, gives, can never be
seen. It is not " a mind-illumined
face." " The body does not charm,
because the mind is seen," but just the
contrary; and if caught by it a man
marries a woman thus disguised, he
may chance not to be satisfied with her
real person. A made-up face may
strike visitors, but will certainly disgust
domestic friends. And one obvious
inference is drawn, truth is not expected to govern the inhabitant of so artificial a form. The false life with which
rouge animates the eyes, is not of the

moſt delicate kind ; nor does a woman's dreſſing herſelf in a way to at-
tract languiſhing glances, give us the
moſt advantageous opinion of the purity of her mind.

I forgot to mention powder among
the deceptions. It is a pity that it ſhould
be ſo generally worn. The moſt beautiful ornament of the features is diſguiſ-
ed, and the ſhade it would give to the
countenance entirely loſt. The color
of every perſon's hair generally ſuits
the complexion, and is calculated to
ſet it off. What abſurdity then do
they run into, who uſe red, blue, and
yellow powder!—And what a falſe
taſte does it exhibit!

The

The quantity of pomatum is often diſguſting. We laugh at the Hottentots, and in ſome things adopt their cuſtoms.

Simplicity of Dreſs, and unaffected manners, ſhould go together. They demand reſpect, and will be admired by people of taſte, even when love is out of the queſtion.

THE

The FINE ARTS.

MUSIC and painting, and many other ingenious arts, are now brought to great perfection, and afford the moſt rational and delicate pleaſure.

It is eaſy to find out if a young perſon has a taſte for them. If they have, do not ſuffer it to lie dormant. Heaven kindly beſtowed it, and a great bleſſing it is; but, like all other bleſſings, may be perverted: yet the intrinſic value is not leſſened by the perverſion. Should nature have been a niggard to them in this reſpect, perſuade them

them to be silent, and not feign raptures they do not feel; for nothing can be more ridiculous.

In music I prefer expression to execution. The simple melody of some artless airs has often soothed my mind, when it has been harrassed by care; and I have been raised from the very depths of sorrow, by the sublime harmony of some of Handel's compositions. I have been lifted above this little scene of grief and care, and mused on Him, from whom all bounty flows.

A person must have sense, taste, and sensibility, to render their music interesting.

refting. The nimble dance of the fingers may raife wonder, but not delight.

As to drawing, thofe cannot be really charmed by it, who do not obferve the beauties of nature, and even admire them.

If a perfon is fond of tracing the effects of the paffions, and marking the appearances they give to the countenance, they will be glad to fee characters difplayed on canvafs, and enter into the fpirit of them ; but if by them the book of nature has not been read, their admiration is childifh.

Works

Works of fancy are very amusing, if a girl has a lively fancy; but if she makes others do the greatest part of them, and only wishes for the credit of doing them, do not encourage her.

Writing may be termed a fine art; and, I am sure, it is a very useful one. The style in particular deserves atten-tion. Young people are very apt to substitute words for sentiments, and clothe mean thoughts in pompous dic-tion. Industry and time are necessary to cure this, and will often do it. Children should be led into correspon-dences, and methods adopted to make them write down their sentiments, and

they

they ſhould be prevailed on to relate the ſtories they have read in their own words. Writing well is of great conſequence in life as to our temporal intereſt, and of ſtill more to the mind; as it teaches a perſon to arrange their thoughts, and digeſt them. Beſides, it forms the only true baſis of rational and elegant converſation.

Reading, and ſuch arts as have been already mentioned, would fill up the time, and prevent a young perſon's being loſt in diſſipation, which enervates the mind, and often leads to improper connections. When habits are fixed, and a character in ſome meaſure formed, the entering into the buſy bufy world, fo far from being dangerous, is ufeful. Knowledge will imperceptibly be acquired, and the tafte improved, if admiration is not more fought for than improvement. For thofe feldom make obfervation who are full of themfelves.

READING.

READING.

IT is an old, but a very true obfervation, that the human mind muft
ever be employed. A relifh for reading, or any of the fine arts, fhould be
cultivated very early in life; and thofe
who reflect can tell, of what importance it is for the mind to have fome re-
fource in itfelf, and not to be entirely
dependant on the fenfes for employment and amufement. If it unfortu-
nately is fo, it muft fubmit to mean-
nefs, and often to vice, in order to
gratify them. The wifeft and beft are
too much under their influence; and
the endeavouring to conquer them,

when

when reaſon and virtue will not give
their ſanction, conſtitutes great part of
the warfare of life. What ſupport,
then, have they who are all ſenſes,
and who are full of ſchemes, which
terminate in temporal objects?

Reading is the moſt rational employment, if people ſeek food for the
underſtanding, and do not read merely
to remember words; or with a view
to quote celebrated authors, and re-
tail ſentiments they do not underſtand
or feel. Judicious books enlarge the
mind and improve the heart, though
ſome, by them, " are made coxcombs
" whom nature meant for fools."

E.   Thoſe

Thofe productions which give a wrong account of the human paffions, and the various accidents of life, ought not to be read before the judgment is formed, or at leaft exercifed. Such accounts are one great caufe of the affectation of young women. Senfibility is defcribed and praifed, and the effects of it reprefented in a way fo different from nature, that thofe who imitate it muft make themfelves very ridiculous. A falfe tafte is acquired, and fenfible books appear dull and infipid after thofe fuperficial performances, which obtain their full end if they can keep the mind in a continual ferment. Gallantry is made the only interefting

fubject

subject with the novelist; reading, therefore, will often co-operate to make his fair admirers infignificant.

I do not mean to recommend books of an abstracted or grave caft. There are in our language many, in which inftruction and amusement are blended; the Adventurer is of this kind. I mention this book on account of its beautiful allegories and affecting tales, and fimilar ones may eafily be felected. Reafon ftrikes moft forcibly when illuftrated by the brilliancy of fancy. The fentiments which are fcattered may be obferved, and when they are relifhed, and the

mind

mind set to work, it may be allowed
to chuse books for itself, for every
thing will then instruct.

I would have every one try to form
an opinion of an author themselves,
though modesty may restrain them
from mentioning it. Many are so
anxious to have the reputation of
taste, that they only praise the authors
whose merit is indisputable. I am sick
of hearing of the sublimity of Milton,
the elegance and harmony of Pope, and
the original, untaught genius of Shake-
spear. These cursory remarks are
made by some who know nothing of
nature, and could not enter into the
                                        spirit

spirit of thofe authors, or underftand them.

A florid ftyle moftly paffes with the ignorant for fine writing ; many fentences are admired that have no meaning in them, though they contain " words of thundering found," and others that have nothing to recommend them but fweet and mufical terminations.

Books of theology are not calculated for young perfons; religion is beft taught by example. The Bible fhould be read with particular refpect, and they fhould not be taught reading by

E 3   fo

so sacred a book ; lest they might consider that as a task, which ought to be
a source of the most exalted satisfaction.

It may be observed, that I recommend the mind's being put into a proper train, and then left to itself.   Fixed
rules cannot be given, it must depend
on the nature and strength of the understanding ; and those who observe
it can best tell what kind of cultiva-
tion will improve it.   The mind is not,
cannot be created by the teacher,
though it may be cultivated, and its
real powers found out.

The active spirits of youth may
make time glide away without intel-
                              lectual

lectual enjoyments ; but when the novelty of the scene is worn off, the want
of them will be felt, and nothing else
can fill up the void. The mind is
confined to the body, and must sink
into sensuality ; for it has nothing to
do but to provide for it, " how it shall
eat and drink, and wherewithal it shall
be clothed."

All kinds of refinement have been
found fault with for increasing our
cares and sorrows ; yet surely the
contrary effect also arises from them.
Taste and thought open many sources
of pleasure, which do not depend on
fortune.

No employment of the mind is a
sufficient excuse for neglecting domeftic duties, and I cannot conceive that
they are incompatible. A woman
may fit herself to be the companion
and friend of a man of fenfe, and yet
know how to take care of his family.

BOARD-

BOARDING-SCHOOLS.

IF a mother has leifure and good fenfe, and more than one daughter, I think fhe could beft educate them herfelf; but as many family reafons render it neceffary fometimes to fend them from home, boarding-fchools are fixed on. I muft own it is my opinion, that the manners are too much attended to in all fchools; and in the nature of things it cannot be otherwife, as the reputation of the houfe depends upon it, and moft people can judge of them. The temper is neglected, the fame leffons are taught to all, and fome get a fmatter-

ing

ing of things they have not capacity
ever to underſtand; few things are
learnt thoroughly, but many follies
contracted, and an immoderate fondneſs for dreſs among the reſt.

To prepare a woman to fulfil the
important duties of a wife and mother, are certainly the objects that
ſhould be in view during the early
period of life; yet accompliſhments
are moſt thought of, and they, and all-
powerful beauty, generally gain the
heart; and as the keeping of it is not
conſidered of until it is loſt, they are
deemed of the moſt conſequence.   A
ſenſible governeſs cannot attend to the
                                          minds

minds of the number she is obliged to
have. She may have been many years
struggling to get established, and when
fortune smiles, does not chuse to lose
the opportunity of providing for old
age; therefore continues to enlarge her
school, with a view to accumulate a
competency for that purpose. Domestic concerns cannot possibly be
made a part of their employment, or
proper converfations often entered on.
Improper books will by stealth be introduced, and the bad example of
one or two vicious children, in the
play-hours, infect a number. Their
gratitude and tendernefs are not called
forth in the way they might be by
maternal

maternal affection. Many miseries does a girl of a mild disposition suffer, which a tender parent could guard her from. I shall not contest about the graces, but the virtues are best learnt at home, if a mother will give up her time and thoughts to the task; but if she cannot, they should be sent to school; for people who do not manage their children well, and have not large fortunes, must leave them often with servants, where they are in danger of still greater corruptions.

The

The TEMPER.

THE forming of the temper ought to be the continual thought, and the first task of a parent or teacher. For to speak moderately, half the miseries of life arise from peevishness, or a tyrannical domineering temper. The tender, who are so by nature, or those whom religion has moulded with so heavenly a disposition, give way for the sake of peace—yet still this giving way undermines their domestic comfort, and stops the current of affection; they labor for patience, and labor is ever painful.

The

The governing of our temper is truly the buſineſs of our whole lives; but ſurely it would very much aſſiſt us if we were early put into the right road. As it is, when reaſon gains ſome ſtrength, ſhe has mountains of rubbiſh to remove, or perhaps exerts all her powers to juſtify the errors of folly and paſſion, rather than root them out.

A conſtant attention to the management of the temper produces gentleneſs and humility, and is practiſed on all occaſions, as it is not done " to be ſeen of men." This meek ſpirit ariſes from good ſenſe and reſolution, and ſhould not be confounded with indolence

lence and timidity; weaknesses of mind,
which often pass for good nature. She
who submits, without conviction, to a
parent or husband, will as unreason-
ably tyrannise over her servants; for
slavish fear and tyranny go together.
Resentment, indeed, may and will be
felt occasionally by the best of human
beings; yet humility will soon conquer it, and convert scorn and contempt into pity, and drive out that
hasty pride which is always guarding
Self from insult; which takes fire on the
most trivial occasions, and which will not
admit of a superior, or even an equal.
With such a temper is often joined
that bashful aukwardness which arises
from

from ignorance, and is frequently termed diffidence; but which does not, in
my opinion, deserve such a distinction.
True humility is not innate, but like
every other good quality must be cultivated. Reflections on miscarriages
of conduct, and mistakes in opinion,
sink it deep into the mind; especially
if those miscarriages and mistakes have
been a cause of pain—when we smart
for our folly we remember it.

Few people look into their own
hearts, or think of their tempers,
though they severely censure others,
on whose side they say the fault always
lies. Now I am apt to believe, that
there

there is not a temper in the world
which does not need correction, and
of courfe attention. Thofe who are
termed good-humored, are frequently giddy, indolent, and infenfible; yet
becaufe the fociety they mix with appear feldom difpleafed with a perfon
who does not conteft, and will laugh
off an affront, they imagine themfelves
pleafing, when they are only not difagreeable. Warm tempers are too
eafily irritated. The one requires a
fpur, the other a rein. Health of
mind, as well as body, muft in general
be obtained by patient fubmiffion to
felf-denial, and difagreeable opera-
tions.

F

If

If the prefence of the Deity be inculcated and dwelt on till an habitual reverence is eftablifhed in the mind, it will check the fallies of anger and fneers of peevifhnefs, which corrode our peace, and render us wretched, without any claim to pity.

The wifdom of the Almighty has fo ordered things, that one caufe produces many effects. While we are looking into another's mind, and forming their temper, we are infenfibly correcting our own; and every act of benevolence which we exert to our fellow-creatures, does ourfelves the moft effential fervices. Active virtue

fits

fits us for the fociety of more exalted beings. Our philanthrophy is a proof, we are told, that we are capable of loving our Creator. Indeed this divine love, or charity, appears to me the principal trait that remains of the illuftrious image of the Deity, which was originally ftampt on the foul, and which is to be renewed. Exalted views will raife the mind above trifling cares, and the many little weakneffes, which make us a torment to ourfelves and others. Our temper will gradually improve, and vanity, which " the creature is made fubject to," has not an entire dominion.

F 2

But

But I have digreſſed.   A judicious parent can only manage a child in this important article; and example will beſt enforce precept.

Be careful, however, not to make hypocrites; ſmothered flames will blaze out with more violence for having been kept down.   Expect not to do all yourſelf; experience muſt enable the child to aſſiſt you; you can only lay the foundation, or prevent bad propenſities from ſettling into habits.

U n-

UNFORTUNATE SITUATION OF FE-
MALES, FASHIONABLY EDUCATED,
AND LEFT WITHOUT A FORTUNE.

I HAVE hitherto only spoken of those
females, who will have a provision
made for them by their parents.   But
many who have been well, or at least
fashionably educated, are left without
a fortune, and if they are not entirely
devoid of delicacy, they must frequently remain single.

Few are the modes of earning a sub-
sistence, and those very humiliating.
Perhaps to be an humble companion
to some rich old cousin, or what is still
F 3   worse,

worſe, to live with ſtrangers, who are ſo intolerably tyrannical, that none of their own relations can bear to live with them, though they ſhould even expect a fortune in reverſion. It is impoſſible to enumerate the many hours of anguiſh ſuch a perſon muſt ſpend. Above the ſervants, yet conſidered by them as a ſpy, and ever reminded of her inferiority when in converſation with the ſuperiors. If ſhe cannot condeſcend to mean flattery, ſhe has not a chance of being a favorite; and ſhould any of the viſitors take notice of her, and ſhe for a moment forget her ſubordinate ſtate, ſhe is ſure to be reminded of it.

Pain-

Painfully fenfible of unkindnefs, fhe is alive to every thing, and many far-cafms reach her, which were perhaps directed another way. She is alone, fhut out from equality and confidence, and the concealed anxiety impairs her conftitution ; for fhe muft wear a cheerful face, or be difmiffed. The being dependant on the caprice of a fellow-creature, though certainly very neceffary in this ftate of difcipline, is yet a very bitter corrective, which we would fain fhrink from.

A teacher at a fchool is only a kind of upper fervant, who has more work than the menial ones.

F 4   A go-

A governess to young ladies is equally difagreeable. It is ten to one if they meet with a reafonable mother; and if fhe is not fo, fhe will be conti-nually finding fault to prove fhe is not ignorant, and be difpleafed if her pupils do not improve, but angry if the proper methods are taken to make them do fo. The children treat them with difrefpect, and often with info-lence. In the mean time life glides away, and the fpirits with it; " and when youth and genial years are flown," they have nothing to fubfift on; or, perhaps, on fome extraordi-nary occafion, fome fmall allowance may be made for them, which is thought a great charity.

The

The few trades which are left, are now gradually falling into the hands of the men, and certainly they are not very refpectable.

It is hard for a perfon who has a relifh for polifhed fociety, to herd with the vulgar, or to condefcend to mix with her former equals when fhe is confidered in a different light.   What unwelcome heart-breaking knowledge is then poured in on her ! I mean a view of the felfifhnefs and depravity of the world ; for every other acquirement is a fource of pleafure, though they may occafion temporary inconveniences.   How cutting is the contempt

tempt she meets with!—A young mind looks round for love and friendship; but love and friendship fly from poverty: expect them not if you are poor! The mind must then sink into meanness, and accommodate itself to its new state, or dare to be unhappy. Yet I think no reflecting person would give up the experience and improvement they have gained, to have avoided the misfortunes; on the contrary, they are thankfully ranked amongst the choicest blessings of life, when we are not under their immediate pressure.

How earnestly does a mind full of sensibility look for disinterested friendship,

2

ship, and long to meet with good un-
alloyed. When fortune smiles they
hug the dear delusion ; but dream not
that it is one. The painted cloud dif-
appears suddenly, the scene is chang-
ed, and what an aching void is left in
the heart! a void which only religion
can fill up—and how few seek this
internal comfort!

A woman, who has beauty without
sentiment, is in great danger of being
seduced ; and if she has any, cannot
guard herself from painful mortifica-
tions. It is very disagreeable to keep
up a continual reserve with men she
has been formerly familiar with ; yet
if

if fhe places confidence, it is ten to
one but fhe is deceived. Few men
ferioufly think of marrying an inferior;
and if they have honor enough not to
take advantage of the artlefs tendernefs of a woman who loves, and thinks
not of the difference of rank, they do
not undeceive her until fhe has antici-
pated happinefs, which, contrafted with
her dependant fituation, appears delightful. The difappointment is fevere; and the heart receives a wound
which does not eafily admit of a com-
pleat cure, as the good that is miffed
is not valued according to its real
worth: for fancy drew the picture,
and grief delights to create food to
feed on.

If

If what I have written fhould be read by parents, who are now going on in thoughtlefs extravagance, and anxious only that their daughters may be *genteelly educated*, let them confider to what forrows they expofe them ; for I have not over-coloured the picture.

Though I warn parents to guard againft leaving their daughters to encounter fo much mifery ; yet if a young woman falls into it, fhe ought not to be difcontented. Good muft ultimately arife from every thing, to thofe who look beyond this infancy of their being ; and here the comfort of a good confcience is our only ftable fupport. The main bufinefs of our lives is to

learn

learn to be virtuous; and He who is training us up for immortal blifs, knows beft what trials will contribute to make us fo; and our refignation and improvement will render us refpectable to ourfelves, and to that Being, whofe approbation is of more value than life itfelf. It is true, tribulation produces anguifh, and we would fain avoid the bitter cup, though convinced its effects would be the moft falutary. The Almighty is then the kind parent, who chaftens and educates, and indulges us not when it would tend to our hurt. He is compaffion itfelf, and never wounds but to heal, when the ends of correction are anfwered.

L O V E.

L O V E.

I THINK there is not a subject that admits so little of reasoning on as love; nor can rules be laid down that will not appear to lean too much one way or the other. Circumstances must, in a great measure, govern the conduct in this particular; yet who can be a judge in their own case? Perhaps, before they begin to consider the matter, they see through the medium of passion, and its suggestions are often mistaken for those of reason. We can no other way account for the absurd matches we every day have an opportunity of observing; for in this

respect,

respect, even the most sensible men and women err. A variety of causes will occasion an attachment; an endeavour to supplant another, or being by some accident confined to the society of one person. Many have found themselves entangled in an affair of honor, who only meant to fill up the heavy hours in an amusing way, or raise jealousy in some other bosom.

It is a difficult task to write on a subject when our own passions are likely to blind us. Hurried away by our feelings, we are apt to set those things down as general maxims, which only our partial experience gives rise to.

to. Though it is not eafy to fay how a perfon fhould act under the immediate influence of paffion, yet they certainly have no excufe who are actuated only by vanity, and deceive by an equivocal behaviour in order to gratify it. There are quite as many male coquets as female, and they are far more pernicious pefts to fociety, as their fphere of action is larger, and they are lefs expofed to the cenfure of the world. A fmothered figh, downcaft look, and the many other little arts which are played off, may give extreme pain to a fincere, artlefs woman, though fhe cannot refent, or complain

G of

of, the injury. This kind of trifling, I think, much more inexcufable than inconftancy; and why it is fo, appears fo obvious, I need not point it out.

People of fenfe and reflection are moft apt to have violent and conftant paffions, and to be preyed on by them. Neither can they, for the fake of prefent pleafure, bear to act in fuch a manner, as that the retrofpect fhould fill them with confufion and regret. Perhaps a delicate mind is not fufceptible of a greater degree of mifery, putting guilt out of the queftion, than what muft arife from the confcioufnefs

of

of loving a perſon whom their reaſon
does not approve. This, I am perſuaded,
has often been the caſe ; and the paſſion muſt either be rooted out, or the
continual allowances and excuſes that
are made will hurt the mind, and leſ-
ſen the reſpect for virtue.   Love, un-
ſupported by eſteem, muſt ſoon expire,
or lead to depravity ; as, on the contrary, when a worthy perſon is the object, it is the greateſt incentive to improvement, and has the beſt effect on
the manners and temper.   We ſhould
always try to fix in our minds the rational grounds we have for loving a
perſon, that we may be able to recollect them when we feel diſguſt or re-

ſent-

fentment; we fhould then habitually
practife forbearance, and the many
petty difputes which interrupt domeftic
peace would be avoided. A woman
cannot reafonably be unhappy, if fhe
is attached to a man of fenfe and
goodnefs, though he may not be all
fhe could wifh.

I am very far from thinking love
irrefiftible, and not to be conquered.
" If weak women go aftray," it is
they, and not the ftars, that are to be
blamed. A refolute endeavour will
almoft always overcome difficulties.
I knew a woman very early in life
warmly attached to an agreeable man,

2   yet

yet fhe faw his faults; his principles were unfixed, and his prodigal turn would have obliged her to have re-ftrained every benevolent emotion of her heart. She exerted her influence to improve him, but in vain did fhe for years try to do it. Convinced of the impoffibility, fhe determined not to marry him, though fhe was forced to encounter poverty and its attendants.

It is too univerfal a maxim with novelifts, that love is felt but once; though it appears to me, that the heart which is capable of receiving an im-preffion at all, and can diftinguifh, will turn to a new object when the firft is

G 3 found

found unworthy. I am convinced it is
practicable, when a respect for goodnefs has the firft place in the mind,
and notions of perfection are not af-
fixed to conftancy. Many ladies are
delicately miferable, and imagine that
they are lamenting the lofs of a lover,
when they are full of felf-applaufe, and
reflections on their own fuperior refinement. Painful feelings are pro-
longed beyond their natural courfe,
to gratify our defire of appearing he-
roines, and we deceive ourfelves as
well as others. When any fudden ftroke
of fate deprives us of thofe we love,
we may not readily get the better of
the blow; but when we find we have

been

been led astray by our passions, and that it was our own imaginations which gave the high colouring to the picture, we may be certain time will drive it out of our minds. For we cannot often think of our folly without being displeased with ourselves, and such reflections are quickly banished. Habit and duty will co-operate, and religion may overcome what reason has in vain combated with; but refinement and romance are often confounded, and sensibility, which occasions this kind of inconstancy, is supposed to have the contrary effect.

Nothing can more tend to deſtroy peace of mind, than platonic attach‑ments. They are begun in falſe re‑finement, and frequently end in ſor‑row, if not in guilt. The two extremes often meet, and virtue carried to ex‑ceſs will ſometimes lead to the oppo‑ſite vice. Not that I mean to inſinuate that there is no ſuch thing as friend‑ſhip between perſons of different ſexes; I am convinced of the contrary. I only mean to obſerve, that if a wo‑man's heart is diſengaged, ſhe ſhould not give way to a pleaſing deluſion, and imagine ſhe will be ſatisfied with the friendſhip of a man ſhe admires, and prefers to the reſt of the world.

The

The heart is very treacherous, and if we do not guard its firſt emotions, we ſhall not afterwards be able to prevent its ſighing for impoſſibilities. If there are any inſuperable bars to an union in the common way, try to diſmiſs the dangerous tenderneſs, or it will under-mine your comfort, and betray you into many errors. To attempt to raiſe ourſelves above human beings is ridiculous; we cannot extirpate our paſ-ſions, nor is it neceſſary that we ſhould, though it may be wiſe ſometimes not to ſtray too near a precipice, leſt we fall over before we are aware. We can-not avoid much vexation and ſorrow, if we are ever ſo prudent; it is then

the

the part of wisdom to enjoy those
gleams of sunshine which do not en-
danger our innocence, or lead to repentance. Love gilds all the prospects
of life, and though it cannot always
exclude apathy, it makes many cares
appear trifling. Dean Swift hated the
world, and only loved particular per-
sons; yet pride rivalled them. A
foolish wish of rising superior to the
common wants and desires of the
human species made him singular, but
not respectable. He sacrificed an amiable woman to his caprice, and made
those shun his company who would
have been entertained and improved
by his conversation, had he loved any
one

one as well as himſelf. Univerſal benevolence is the firſt duty, and we
ſhould be careful not to let any paſſion ſo engroſs our thoughts, as to prevent our practiſing it. After all the
dreams of rapture, earthly pleaſures
will not fill the mind, or ſupport it
when they have not the ſanction of
reaſon, or are too much depended on.
The tumult of paſſion will ſubſide,
and even the pangs of diſappoint-
ment ceaſe to be felt. But for the
wicked there is a worm that never
dies—a guilty conſcience. While that
calm ſatisfaction which reſignation
produces, which cannot be deſcribed,
but

but may be attained, in fome degree, by thofe who try to keep in the ftrait, though thorny path which leads to blifs, fhall fanctify the forrows, and dignify the character of virtue.

MATRI-

MATRIMONY.

EARLY marriages are, in my opinion, a ſtop to improvement. If we were born only " to draw nutrition, propagate and rot," the ſooner the end of creation was anſwered the better; but as women are here allowed to have ſouls, the ſoul ought to be attended to. In youth a woman endeavours to pleaſe the other ſex, in order, generally ſpeaking, to get married, and this endeavour calls forth all her powers. If ſhe has had a tolerable education, the foundation only is laid, for the mind does not ſoon arrive at maturity, and ſhould not be engroſſed groffed by domeftic cares before any habits are fixed. The paffions alfo have too much influence over the judgment to, fuffer it to direct her in this moft important affair; and many women, I am perfuaded, marry a man before they are twenty, whom they would have rejected fome years after. Very frequently, when the education has been neglected, the mind improves itfelf, if it has leifure for reflection, and experience to reflect on; but how can this happen when they are forced to act before they have had time to think, or find that they are unhappily married? Nay, fhould they be fo fortunate as to get a good hufband, they

will

will not set a proper value on him; he will be found much inferior to the lovers described in novels, and their want of knowledge makes them frequently disgusted with the man, when the fault is in human nature.

When a woman's mind has gained some strength, she will in all probability pay more attention to her actions than a girl can be expected to do; and if she thinks seriously, she will chuse for a companion a man of principle; and this perhaps young people do not sufficiently attend to, or see the necessity of doing. A woman of feeling must be very much hurt if she

is

is obliged to keep her children out of
their father's company, that their mo-
rals may not be injured by his converfation; and befides, the whole arduous tafk of education devolves on
her, and in fuch a cafe it is not very
practicable. Attention to the education of children muft be irkfome, when
life appears to have fo many charms,
and its pleafures are not found falla-
cious. Many are but juft returned
from a boarding-fchool, when they
are placed at the head of a family,
and how fit they are to manage it, I
leave the judicious to judge. Can
they improve a child's underftanding,
when they are fcarcely out of the ftate
of childhood themfelves?

Dignity

Dignity of manners, too, and proper reſerve are often wanting. The conſtant attendant on too much familiarity is contempt. Women are often before marriage prudiſh, and afterwards they think they may innocently give way to fondneſs, and overwhelm the poor man with it. They think they have a legal right to his affections, and grow remiſs in their endeavours to pleaſe. There are a thouſand name-leſs decencies which good ſenſe gives riſe to, and artleſs proofs of regard which flow from the heart, and will reach it, if it is not depraved. It has ever occurred to me, that is was ſuf-ficient for a woman to receive careſſes,

H   and

and not beſtow them. She ought to diſtinguiſh between fondneſs and ten-derneſs. The latter is the ſweeteſt cordial of life; but, like all other cordials, ſhould be reſerved for particular occaſions; to exhilarate the ſpirits, when depreſſed by ſickneſs, or loſt in ſorrow. Senſibility will beſt inſtruct. Some delicacies can never be pointed out or deſcribed, though they ſink deep into the heart, and render the hours of diſtreſs ſupportable.

A woman ſhould have ſo proper a pride, as not eaſily to forget a deliberate affront; though ſhe muſt not too haſtily reſent any little coolneſs. We

We cannot always feel alike, and all are fubject to changes of temper without an adequate caufe.

Reafon muft often be called in to fill up the vacuums of life; but too many of our fex fuffer theirs to lie dormant. A little ridicule and fmart turn of expreffion, often confutes without convincing; and tricks are played off to raife tendernefs, even while they are forfeiting efteem.

Women are faid to be the weaker veffel, and many are the miferies which this weaknefs brings' on them. Men have in fome refpects very much the advantage.

H 2   vantage.

vantage. If they have a tolerable underftanding, it has a chance to be cultivated. They are forced to fee human nature as it is, and are not left to
dwell on the pictures of their own imaginations. Nothing, I am fure, calls
forth the faculties fo much as the being obliged to ftruggle with the world;
and this is not a woman's province in
a married ftate. Her fphere of action
is not large, and if fhe is not taught to
look into her own heart, how trivial
are her occupations and purfuits!
What little arts engrofs and narrow
her mind! " Cunning fills up the
mighty void of fenfe;" and cares,
which do not improve the heart or un

derftand

derftanding, take up her attention.
Of courfe, fhe falls a prey to childifh
anger, and filly capricious humors,
which render her rather infignificant
than vicious.

In a comfortable fituation, a cultivated mind is neceffary to render a
woman contented; and in a miferable
one, it is her only confolation. A fenfible, delicate woman, who by fome
ftrange accident, or miftake, is joined
to a fool or a brute, muft be wretched
beyond all names of wretchednefs, if
her views are confined to the prefent
fcene. Of what importance, then, is
intellectual improvement, when our

H 3 com-

comfort here, and happineſs hereafter, depends upon it.

Principles of religion ſhould be fixed, and the mind not left to fluctuate in the time of diſtreſs, when it can receive ſuccour from no other quarter. The conviction that every thing is working for our good will ſcarcely produce reſignation, when we are deprived of our deareſt hopes. How they can be ſatisfied, who have not this conviction, I cannot conceive; I rather think they will turn to ſome worldly ſupport, and fall into folly, if not vice. For a little refinement only leads a woman into the wilds of romance,

mance, if she is not religious; nay, more, there is no true sentiment without it, nor perhaps any other effectual check to the passions.

DE-

DESULTORY THOUGHTS.

AS every kind of domeſtic concern and family buſineſs is properly a woman's province, to enable her to diſcharge her duty ſhe ſhould ſtudy the different branches of it. Nothing is more uſeful in a family than a little knowledge of phyſic, ſufficient to make the miſtreſs of it a judicious nurſe. Many a perſon, who has had a ſenſible phyſician to attend them, have been loſt for want of the other; for tenderneſs, without judgment, ſometimes does more harm than good.

The ignorant imagine there is ſomething very myſterious in the practice
of

of phyfic. They expect a medicine to work like a charm, and know nothing of the progrefs and crifis of diforders. The keeping of the patient low appears cruel, all kind of regimen is difregarded, and though the fever rages, they cannot be perfuaded not to give them inflammatory food. " How (fay they) can a perfon get well without nourifhment?"

The mind, too, fhould be foothed at the fame time; and indeed, whenever it finks, foothing is, at firft, better than reafoning. The flackened nerves are not to be braced by words. When a mind is worried by care, or oppreffed

by

by forrow, it cannot in a moment
grow tranquil, and attend to the voice
of reafon.

St. Paul fays, " No chaftening for
the prefent feemeth to be joyous ; but
grievous : neverthelefs, afterwards it
yieldeth the peaceable fruits of righte-
oufnefs unto them which are exercifed
thereby." It is plain, from thefe
words of the Apoftle, and from many
other parts of Scripture, that afflictions are neceffary to teach us true
wifdom, and that in fpite of this conviction, men would fain avoid the
bitter draught, though certain that the
drinking of it would be conducive to
the

the purifying of their hearts. He who made us muft know what will tend to our ultimate good ; yet ftill all this is grievous, and the heart will throb with anguifh when deprived of what it loves, and the tongue can fcarcely faulter out an acquiefcence to the Divine Will, when it is fo contrary to our own. Due allowance ought then to be made for human infirmities, and the unhappy fhould be confidered as objects of com-paffion, rather than blame. But in a very different ftile does confolatory advice generally run ; for inftead of pouring oil or wine into the wound, it tends to convince the unfortunate perfons that they are weak as well as unhappy.

I am

I am apt to imagine, that forrow and refignation are not incompatible; and that though religion cannot make fome difappointments pleafant, it prevents our repining, even while we fmart under them. Did our feelings and reafon always coincide, our paffage through this world could not juftly be termed a warfare, and faith would no longer be a virtue. It is our preferring the things that are not feen, to thofe which are, that proves us to be the heirs of promife.

On the facred word of the Moft High, we rely with firm affurance, that the fufferings of the prefent life will

will work out a far more exceeding
and eternal weight of glory; yet ſtill
they are allowed to be afflictions,
which, though temporary, muſt ſtill
be grievous.

The difference between thoſe who
ſorrow without hope, and thoſe who
look up to Heaven, is not that the
one feel more than the other, for they
may be both equally depreſſed.; but
the latter think of the peaceable fruits
which are to reſult from the diſcipline, and therefore patiently ſubmit.

I have almoſt run into a ſermon,—
and I ſhall not make an apology for it.
                                    What-

Whatever contributes to make us compassionate and resolute, is of the utmost consequence; both these qualities are necessary, if we are confined to a sick chamber. Various are the misfortunes of life, and it may be the lot of most of us to see death in all its terrors, when it attacks a friend; yet even then we must exert our friendship, and try to chear the departing spirit.

THE

THE BENEFITS WHICH ARISE FROM DISAPPOINMENTS.

MOST women, and men too, have no character at all. Juft opinions and virtuous paffions appear by ftarts, and while we are giving way to the love and admiration which thofe qualities raife, they are quite different creatures. It is reflection which forms habits, and fixes principles indelibly on the heart; without it, the mind is like a wreck drifted about by every fquall. The paffion that we think moft of will foon rival all the reft; it is then in our power, this way, to ftrengthen our

good

good difpofitions, and in fome meafure
to eftablifh a character, which will not
depend on every accidental impulfe.
To be convinced of truths, and yet
not to feel or act up to them, is a
common thing. Prefent pleafure drives
all before it, and adverfity is merci-
fully fent to force us to think.

In the fchool of adverfity we learn
knowledge as well as virtue; yet we
lament our hard fate, dwell on our difappointments, and never confider that
our own wayward minds, and incon-
fiftent hearts, require thefe needful
correctives. Medicines are not fent
to perfons in health.

It

It is a well-known remark, that our very wishes give us not our wish. I have often thought it might be set down as a maxim, that the greatest disappointment we can meet with is the gratification of our fondest wishes. But truth is sometimes not pleasant ; we turn from it, and doat on an illusion ; and if we were not in a probationary state, we should do well to thicken the cloud, rather than dispel it.

There are some who delight in observing moral beauty, and their souls sicken when forced to view crimes and follies which could never hurt them. How numerous are the sorrows which

I   reach

reach such bosoms! They may truly be called *human creatures*; on every side they touch their fellow-mortals, and vibrate to the touch. Common humanity points out the important duties of our station; but sensibility (a kind of instinct, strengthened by reflection) can only teach the numberless minute things which give pain or pleasure.

A benevolent mind often suffers more than the object it commiserates, and will bear an inconvenience itself to shelter another from it. It makes allowance for failings though it longs to meet perfection, which it seems

formed

formed to adore. The Author of all good continually calls himſelf, a God long-ſuffering; and thoſe moſt reſemble him who practiſe forbearance. Love and compaſſion are the moſt delightful feelings of the ſoul, and to exert them to all that breathe is the wiſh of the benevolent heart. To ſtruggle with ingratitude and ſelfiſhneſs is grating beyond expreſſion: and the ſenſe we have of our weakneſs, though uſeful, is not pleaſant. Thus it is with us, when we look for happineſs, we meet with vexations: and if, now and then, we give way to tenderneſs, or any of the amiable paſſions, and taſte pleaſure, the mind, ſtrained beyond its

uſual

usual tone, falls into apathy.   And yet we were made to be happy! But our passions will not contribute much to our bliss, till they are under the dominion of reason, and till that reason is enlightened and improved.   Then sighing will cease, and all tears will be wiped away by that Being, in whose presence there is fulness of joy.

A person of tenderness must ever have particular attachments, and ever be disappointed; yet still they must be attached, in spite of human frailty; for if the mind is not kept in motion by either hope or fear, it sinks into the dreadful state before-mentioned.

I have

I have very often heard it made a ſubject of ridicule, that when a perſon is diſappointed in this world, they turn to the next. Nothing can be more natural than the tranſition; and it ſeems to me the ſcheme of Providence, that our finding things unſatisfactory here, ſhould force us to think of the better country to which we are going.

I 3   O N

ON THE TREATMENT OF SERVANTS.

THE management of servants is a great part of the employment of a woman's life; and her own temper depends very much on her behaviour to them.

Servants are, in general, ignorant and cunning; we must consider their characters, if we would treat them properly, and continually practise forbearance. The same methods we use with children may be adopted with regard to them. Act uniformly, and never find fault without a just cause;

and

and when there, is, be positive, but not
angry. A mind that is not too much
engrossed by trifles, will not be discom-
posed by every little domestic disaster ;
and a thinking person can very readily
make allowance for those faults which
arise from want of reflection and education. I have seen the peace of a
whole family disturbed by some trivial,
cross accident, and hours spent in use-
less upbraidings about some mistake
which would never have been thought
of, but for the consequences that arose
from it. An error in judgment or an
accident should not be severely repre-
hended. It is a proof of wisdom to

I 4   profit

profit by experience, and not lament irremediable evils.

A benevolent perſon muſt ever wiſh to ſee thoſe around them comfortable, and try to be the cauſe of that comfort. The wide difference which education makes, I ſhould ſuppoſe, would prevent familiarity in the way of equality; yet kindneſs muſt be ſhewn, if we are deſirous that our domeſtics ſhould be attached to our intereſt and perſons. How pleaſing it is to be attended with a ſmile of willingneſs, to be conſulted when they are at a loſs, and looked up to as a friend and benefactor when they are in diſtreſs. It

3   is

is true we may often meet with ingratitude, but it ought not to difcourage us; the refrefhing fhowers of heaven fertilize the fields of the unworthy, as well as the juft. We fhould nurfe them in illnefs, and our fuperior judgment in thofe matters would often alleviate their pains.

Above all, we owe them a good example. The ceremonials of religion, on their account, fhould be attended to; as they always reverence them to a fuperftitious degree, or elfe neglect them. We fhould not fhock the faith of the meaneft fellow-creature; nay more, we fhould comply

with

with their prejudices; for their religious notions are so over-run with them, that they are not easily separated; and by trying to pluck up the tares, we may root up the wheat with them.

The woman who gives way to caprice and ill-humour in the kitchen, cannot easily smooth her brow when her husband returns to his fire-side; nay, he may not only see the wrinkles of anger, but hear the disputes at second-hand. I heard a Gentleman, say, it would break any man's heart to hear his wife argue such a case. Men who are employed about things of

confe-

confequence, think thefe affairs more infignificant than they really are; for the warmth with which we engage in any bufinefs increafes its importance, and our not entering into them has the contrary effect.

The behaviour of girls to fervants. is generally in extremes; too fami-liar or haughty. Indeed the one often produces the other, as a check, when the freedoms are troublefome.

We cannot make our fervants wife or good, but we may teach them to be decent and orderly; and order leads to fome degree of morality.

THE

THE OBSERVANCE OF SUNDAY.

THE inſtitution of keeping the ſeventh day holy was wiſely or-dered by Providence for two purpoſes. To reſt the body, and call off the mind from the too eager purſuit of the ſhadows of this life, which, I am afraid, often obſcure the proſpect of futurity, and fix our thoughts on earth. A reſpect for this ordinance is, I am perſuaded, of the utmoſt conſequence to national religion. The vulgar have ſuch a notion of it, that with them, going to church, and being religious, are almoſt ſynonymous terms. They

are

are fo loft in their fenfes, that if this
day did not continually remind them,
they would foon forget that there was
a God in the world. Some forms are
neceffary to fupport vital religion, and
without them it would foon languifh,
and at laft expire.

It is unfortunate, that this day is
either kept with puritanical exactnefs,
which renders it very irkfome, or loft
in diffipation and thoughtleffnefs. Either way is very prejudicial to the
minds of children and fervants, who
ought not to be let run wild, nor
confined too ftrictly; and, above all,
fhould not fee their parents or mafters
                                    indulge

indulge themselves in things which are generally thought wrong. I am fully persuaded, that servants have such a notion of card-playing, that wherever it is practised of a Sunday their minds are hurt; and the barrier between good and evil in some measure broken down. Servants, who are accustomed to bodily labour, will fall into as laborious pleasures, if they are not gently restrained, and some substitute found out for them.

Such a close attention to a family may appear to many very disagreeable; but the path of duty will be found pleasant after some time; and the

the paffions being employed this way,
will, by degrees, come under the fub-
jection of reafon. I mean not to be
rigid, the obftructions which arife in
the way of our duty, do not ftrike a
fpeculatift; I know, too, that in the
moment of action, even a well-difpofed
mind is often carried away by the
prefent impulfe, and that it requires
fome experience to be able to diftinguifh the dictates of reafon from thofe
of paffion. The truth is feldom found
out until the tumult is over; we then
wake as from a dream, and when we
furvey what we have done, and feel
the folly of it, we might call on reafon and fay, why fleepeft thou? Yet
though

though people are led aftray by their paffions, and even relapfe after the moft bitter repentance, they fhould not defpair, but ftill try to regain the right road, and cultivate fuch habits as may affift them.

I never knew much focial virtue to refide in a houfe where the fabbath was grofsly violated.

ON

ON THE MISFORTUNE OF FLUCTUATING PRINCIPLES.

IF we look for any comfort in friend-ship or society, we muſt aſſociate with thoſe who have fixed principles with reſpeſt to religion; for without them, repeated experience convinces me, the moſt ſhining qualities are un-ſtable, and not to be depended on.

It has often been a matter of ſur-priſe to me, that ſo few people exa-mine the tenets of the religion they profeſs, or are chriſtians through con-viſtion. They have no anchor to reſt on, nor any fixed chart to direſt them

K

in

in the doubtful voyage of life; how then can they hope to find the " haven of reft ?" But they think not of it, and cannot be expected to forego prefent advantages. Noble actions muft arife from noble thoughts and views ; when they are confined to this world, they muft be groveling.

Faith, with refpect to the promife of eternal happinefs, can only enable us to combat with our paffions, with a chance of victory. There are many who pay no attention to revelation, and more, perhaps, who have not any fixed belief in it. The fure word of comfort is neglected ; and how people

3   can

can live without it, I can fcarcely
conceive. For as the fun renews the
face of nature, and chafes away dark-
nefs from the world, fo does this, ftill
greater bleffing, have the fame effect
on the mind, and enlightens and cheers
it when every thing elfe fails.

A true fenfe of our infirmities is the
way to make us chriftians in the moft
extenfive fenfe of the word. A mind
depreffed with a weight of weakneffes
can only find comfort in the promifes
of the Gofpel. The affiftance there
offered muft raife the humble foul;
and the account of the atonement
that has been made, gives a rational

K 2   ground

ground for resting in hope until the toil of virtue is over, and faith has nothing to be exercised on.

It is the fashion now for young men to be deists. And many a one has improper books sent adrift in a sea of doubts—of which there is no end. This is not a land of certainty; there is no confining the wandering reason, and but one clue to prevent its being lost in endless researches. Reason is indeed the heaven-lighted lamp, in man, and may safely be trusted, when not entirely depended on; but when it pretends to discover what is beyond its ken, it certainly stretches
the

the line too far, and runs into abfur-
dity. Some fpeculations are idle and
others hurtful, as they raife pride, and
turn the thoughts to fubjects that
ought to be left unexplored. With
love and awe we fhould think of the
High and Lofty One, that inhabiteth
eternity! and not prefume to fay how
He muft exift who created us. How
unfortunate it is, that man muft fink
into a brute, and not employ his mind,
or elfe, by thinking, grow fo proud,
as often to imagine himfelf a fuperior being! It is not the doubts of
profound thinkers that I here allude
to, but the crude notions which young
men fport away when together, and

K 3　　　　　fome-sometimes in the company of young women, to make them wonder at their superior wisdom! There cannot be any thing more dangerous to a mind, not accustomed to think, than doubts delivered in a ridiculing way. They never go deep enough to solve them, of course they stick by them; and though they might not influence their conduct, if a fear of the world prevents their being guilty of vices, yet their thoughts are not restrained, and they should be observed diligently, " For out of them are the issues of life." A nice sense of right and wrong ought to be acquired, and then not only great vices will be avoided, but every little meanness; truth will reign

in

in the inward parts, and mercy will attend her.

I have indeed so much compassion for those young females who are entering into the world without fixed principles, that I would fain persuade them to examine a little into the matter. For though in the season of gaiety they may not feel the want of them, in that of distress where will they fly for succour? Even with this support, life is a labor of patience—a conflict; and the utmost we can gain is a small portion of peace, a kind of watchful tranquillity, that is liable to continual interruptions.

K 4   " Then

" Then keep each passion down, however dear;

" Trust me, the tender are the most severe.

" Guard, while 'tis thine, thy philosophic ease,

" And ask no joy but that of virtuous peace;

" That bids defiance to the storms of fate :

" High bliss is only for a higher state."

THOMSON.

BENE-

BENEVOLENCE.

THIS firſt, and moſt amiable virtue, is often found in young
perſons that afterwards grow ſelfiſh;
a knowledge of the arts of others, is
an excuſe to them for practiſing the
ſame; and becauſe they have been
deceived once, or have found objects
unworthy of their charity—if any one
appeals to their feelings, the formida-
ble word Impoſture inſtantly baniſhes
the compaſſionate emotions, and ſi-
lences conſcience. I do not mean to
confine the exerciſe of benevolence to
alms-giving, though it is a very mate-
rial part of it. Faith, hope, and cha-

2   rity,

rity, ought to attend us in our paſſage through this world; but the two firſt leave us when we die, while the other is to be the conſtant inmate of our breaſt through all eternity. We ought not to ſuffer the heavenly ſpark to be quenched by ſelfiſhneſs; if we do, how can we expect it to revive, when the ſoul is diſentangled from the body, and ſhould be prepared for the realms of love? Forbearance and liberality of ſentiment are the virtues of maturity. Children ſhould be taught every thing in a poſitive way; and their own experience can only teach them afterwards to make diſtinctions and allowances. It is then the inferior part of bene-

benevolence that comes within their
fphere of action, and it fhould not be
fuffered to fleep. Some part of the
money that is allowed them for pocket-
money, they fhould be encouraged to
lay out this way, and the fhort-lived
emotions of pity continually retraced
'till they grow into habits.

I knew a child that would, when
very young, fit down and cry if it met
a poor perfon, after it had laid out its
money in cakes; this occurred once
or twice, and the tears were fhed with
additional diftrefs every time; till at
laft it refifted the temptation, and
faved the money.

I think

I think it a very good method for girls to have a certain allowance for cloaths. A mother can eafily, without feeming to do it, obferve how they fpend it, and direct them accordingly. By thefe means they would learn the value of money, and be obliged to contrive. This would be a practical leffon of œconomy fuperior to all the theories that could be thought of. The having a fixed ftipend, too, would enable them to be charitable, in the true fenfe of the word, as they would then give their own ; and by denying themfelves little ornaments, and doing their own work, they might increafe the fum appropriated to charitable purpofes.

A lively

A lively principle of this kind would also overcome indolence; for I have known people wasteful and penurious at the same time; but the wastefulness was to spare themselves trouble, and others only felt the effects of their penury, to make the balance even.

Women too often confine their love and charity to their own families. They fix not in their minds the precedency of moral obligations, or make their feelings give way to duty. Goodwill to all the human race should dwell in our bosoms, nor should love to individuals induce us to violate this first of duties, or make us sacrifice the interest

tereſt of any fellow-creature, to promote that of another, whom we happen
to be more partial to. A parent, under
diſtreſſed circumſtances, ſhould be ſupported, even though it ſhould prevent
our ſaving a fortune for a child ; nay
more, ſhould they be both in diſtreſs
at the ſame time, the prior obligation
ſhould be firſt diſcharged.

Under this head may be included
the treatment of animals. Over them
many children tyrannize with impu-
nity ; and find amuſement in tormenting,
or wantonly killing, any inſect that
comes in their way, though it does
them no injury. I am perſuaded, if
they

they were told ſtories of them, and led
to take an intereſt in their welfare and
occupations, they would be tender to
them ; as it is, they think man the
only thing of conſequence in the creation. I once prevented a girl's killing ants, for ſport, by adapting Mr.
Addiſon's account of them to her underſtanding. Ever after ſhe was careful not to tread on them, leſt ſhe ſhould
diſtreſs the whole community.

Stories of inſects and animals are
the firſt that ſhould rouſe the childiſh
paſſions, and exerciſe humanity ; and
then they will riſe to man, and from
him to his Maker.

CARD-

CARD-PLAYING.

CARD-playing is now the conftant amufement, I may fay employment, of young and old, in genteel life. After all the fatigue of the toilet, blooming girls are fet down to card-tables, and the moft unpleafing paffions called forth. Avarice does not wait for grey hairs and wrinkles, but marks a countenance where the loves and graces ought to revel. The hours that fhould be fpent in improving the mind, or in innocent mirth, are thus thrown away; and if the ftake is not confiderable enough to roufe the paffions, loft in infipidity, and a habit ac-

quired

quired which may lead to serious mischief. Not to talk of gaming, many
people play for more than they can
well afford to lose, and this sours their
temper. Cards are the universal refuge
to which the idle and the ignorant resort, to pass life away, and to keep their
inactive souls awake, by the tumult of
hope and fear.

" Unknown to them, when sensual plea_
" sures cloy,
" To fill the languid pause with finer joy;
" Unknown those powers that raise the soul
" to flame,
" Catch every nerve, and vibrate through
" the frame."

And, of course, this is their favourite
amusement. Silent, stupid attention

L

appears

appears neceſſary; and too frequently little arts are practiſed which debaſe the character, and at beſt give it a trifling turn. Certainly nothing can be more abſurd than permitting girls to acquire a fondneſs for cards. In youth the imagination is lively, and novelty gives charms to every ſcene; pleaſure almoſt obtrudes itſelf, and the pliable mind and warm affections are eaſily wrought on. They want not thoſe reſources, which even reſpectable and ſenſible perſons ſometimes find neceſſary, when they ſee life, as it is unſatisfactory, and cannot anticipate pleaſures, which they know will fade when nearly viewed. Youth

I   is

is the season of activity, and should
not be lost in listlessness. Knowledge
ought to be acquired, a laudable am-
bition encouraged ; and even the errors of passion may produce useful experience, expand the faculties, and
teach them to know their own hearts.
The most shining abilities, and the
most amiable dispositions of the mind,
require culture, and a proper situation,
not only to ripen and improve them,
but to guard them against the perver-
sions of vice, and the contagious influence of bad examples.

L 2   THE

THE THEATRE.

THE amusements which this place afford are generally suppofed the moft rational, and are really fo to a cultivated mind; yet one that is not quite formed may learn affectation at the theatre. Many of our admired tragedies are too full of declamation, and a falfe difplay of the paffions. A heroine is often made to grieve ten or twenty years, and yet the unabated forrow has not given her cheeks a pallid hue; fhe ftill infpires the moft violent paffion in every beholder, and her own yields not to time. The prominent features of a paffion are eafily

4   copied,

copied, while the more delicate touches
are overlooked. That ſtart of Cor-
delia's, when her father ſays, " I
think that Lady is my daughter," has
affected me beyond meaſure, when I
could unmoved hear Caliſta deſcribe
the cave in which ſhe would live
" Until her tears had waſhed her guilt
away."

The principal characters are too
frequently made to riſe above human
nature, or ſink below it; and this occaſions many falſe concluſions. The
chief uſe of dramatic performances
ſhould be to teach us to diſcriminate
characters; but if we reſt in ſeparat-

L 3   ing

ing the good from the bad, we are very fuperficial obfervers. May I venture a conjecture?—I cannot help thinking, that every human creature has fome fpark of goodnefs, which their long-fuffering and benevolent Father gives them an opportunity of improving, though they may perverfely fmother it before they ceafe to breathe.

Death is treated in too flight a manner; and fought, when difappointments occur, with a degree of impatience, which proves that the main end of life has not been confidered. That fearful punifhment of fin, and convulfion of nature, is too often expofed

poſed to public view. Until very
lately I never had the courage even to
look at a perſon dying on the ſtage.
The hour of death is not the time
for the diſplay of paſſions ; nor do I
think it natural it ſhould : the mind
is then dreadfully diſturbed, and the
trifling ſorrows of this world not
thought of. The deaths on the ſtage,
in ſpite of the boaſted ſenſibility of the
age, ſeem to have much the ſame
effect on a polite audience, as the execution of malefactors has on the mob
that follow them to Tyburn.

The worſt ſpecies of immorality is inculcated, and life (which is to determine
the fate of eternity) thrown away when

L 4   a king-

a kingdom or miftrefs is loft. Patience and fubmiffion to the will of
Heaven, and thofe virtues which render us ufeful to fociety, are not brought
forward to view ; nor can they occafion thofe furprifing turns of fortune
which moft delight vulgar minds.
The almoft imperceptible progrefs cf
the paffions, which Shakefpeare has fo
finely delineated, are not fufficiently
obferved, though the ftart of the actor
is applauded. Few tragedies, I think,
will pleafe a perfon of difcernment;
and their fenfibility is fure to be hurt.

Young perfons, who are happily
fituated, do well to enter into ficti-
tious

tious diſtreſs ; and 'if they have any judicious perſon to direct their judg-ment, it may be improved while their hearts are melted. Yet I would not have them confine their compaſſion to the diſtreſſes occaſioned by love ; and perhaps their feelings might more pro-fitably be rouſed, if they were to ſee ſometimes the complicated miſery of ſickneſs and poverty, and weep for the beggar inſtead of the king.

Comedy is not now ſo cenſurable as it was ſome years ago ; and a chaſte ear is not often ſhocked with inde-cencies. When follies are pointed out, and vanity ridiculed, it may be

very

very improving; and perhaps the ſtage is the only place where ridicule is uſeful.

What I have ſaid is certainly only applicable to thoſe who go to ſee the play, and not to ſhew themſelves and waſte time. The moſt inſignificant amuſement will afford inſtruction to thinking minds, and the moſt rational will be loſt on a vacant one.

Remarks on the actors are fre-quently very tireſome. It is a fa-ſhionable topic, and a thread-bare one; it requires great abilities, and a knowledge of nature, to be a com-petent

petent judge; and thofe who do not enter into the fpirit of the author, are not qualified to converfe with confidence on the fubject.

PUBLIC

PUBLIC PLACES.

UNDER this head I rank all those places, which are open to an indiscriminate resort of company. There seems at present such a rage for pleasure, that when adversity does not call home the thoughts, the whole day is mostly spent in preparations and plans, or in actual dissipation. Solitude appears insupportable, and domestic comfort stupid. And though the amusements may not always be relished, the mind is so enervated it cannot exert itself to find out any other substitute. An immoderate fondness for dress is acquired, and many fashionable

able

able females fpend half the night in going from one place to another to difplay their finery, repeat commonplace compliments, and raife envy in their acquaintance whom they endeavour to outfhine. Women, who are engaged in thofe fcenes, muft fpend more time in drefs than they ought to do, and it will occupy their thoughts when they fhould be better employed.

In the fine Lady how few traits do we obferve of thofe affections which dignify human nature! If fhe has any maternal tendernefs, it is of a childifh kind. We cannot be too careful not to verge on this character; though fhe she lives many years she is still a child in understanding, and of so little use to society, that her death would scarcely be observed.

Dissipation leads to poverty, which cannot be patiently borne by those who have lived on the vain applause of others, on account of outward advantages; these were the things they imagined of most consequence, and of course they are tormented with false shame, when by a reverse of fortune they are deprived of them.

A young innocent girl, when she first enters into gay scenes, finds her
spirits

spirits so raised by them, that she would often be lost in delight, if she was not checked by observing the behaviour of a class of females who attend those places. What a painful train of reflections do then arise in the mind, and convictions of the vice and folly of the world are prematurely forced on it. It is no longer a paradise, for innocence is not there; the taint of vice poisons every enjoyment, and affectation, though despised, is very contagious. If these reflections do not occur, languor follows the extraordinary exertions, and weak minds fall a prey to imaginary distress, to banish which they are obliged to take as a remedy what produced the disease.

We

We talk of amufements unbending the mind; fo they ought; yet even in the hours of relaxation we are acquiring habits. A mind accuftomed to obferve can never be quite idle, and will catch improvement on all occafions. Our purfuits and pleafures fhould have the fame tendency, and every thing concur to prepare us for a ftate of purity and happinefs. There vice and folly will not poifon our pleafures; our faculties will expand, and not miftake their objects; and we fhall no longer " fee as through a " glafs darkly, but know, even as we " are known."

F I N I S.